Brief Introduction to Technological Determinism

By

Arghya Ray
B.A., M.C.S.A., C.C.N.A. (from 2008 through 2011)

Table of Contents

Preface

In today's world, technology and society are intricately related to each other. Consequently, studies on technology and society are becoming more and more mutually inclusive. However, there appears to be a chronic lack of academic reference material which can address this development sufficiently. Due to professional and academic reasons, I have studied topics in both technology and social sciences. As a trainee and enthusiast in the field of science and technology, I have found that most of the technical articles used in various training courses address management specific issues. Especially information technology is a subject which extensively deals with the necessities of contemporary business management and communication systems. Nevertheless, it should be kept in mind that both technology experts and business managers are part of the society. Without understanding society, we cannot understand our clients and customers. But if a professional does not know that exactly how technology is related to the society and vice versa, he/she cannot devise technological systems that would benefit the society in the long run. Apparently, study of society and social sciences is not an imperative for a technical or management trainee. But in the age of social networks like Facebook and with increased public focus on topics like corporate social responsibility (CSR), it is not a good idea to neglect the social influence and importance of technology as a whole.

Likewise, students of sociology must not think that they are unlikely to be exposed to technological issues. For example, a sociology scholar may have to research on a topic of social importance with the help of a social networking website such as Facebook or Twitter. Increased use of statistical software like STATA in sociological research projects is another example of how social studies are being aided and improved by technical tools. Consequently, I feel that there should be some academic material that can bridge the existing gap between technological, managerial, and sociological enquiries. Also, professional technology experts, managers, and sociologists may need some refresher academic material to understand the key concepts regarding both technology and society. In my humble opinion, interaction between society and technology must be viewed from a non technical perspective in the first go. The reason is that the academic material or reference note required at this level must be useful to a general audience who might come from various professional and academic fields.

Consequently, I selected technological determinism as an excellent starting point toward abridging the existing gap. Technological determinism can amply help us in developing an understanding on how society and technology interact. The basic framework of this theoretical paradigm has been constructed on the basis of Thorstein B. Veblen's works. Although a strictly deterministic approach might damage the very target of this book, I have focused on the philosophical side of determinism. This has been done to provide a wholesome view of the debates that frequently arise while analyzing the relationships between technology and society. Although this book is primarily meant for sociology students, I have adopted an interdisciplinary approach. If a manager or technology expert wishes to work on socio-technical projects, this book can be helpful for them as well.

Arghya Ray
(October 2013)

Brief Introduction to
Technological Determinism

Introductory Note

The theory of technological determinism has been directly derived as a consequence to Veblen's theory of institutional change (Brette 2003). The concept of institutional change can be mapped onto social change since Veblen's point of view envisaged the human society as a vast and complex institution containing numerous smaller institutions within it. Veblen's technological determinism is based on a reductionist explanation for social changes. Brette (2003) has stated that Veblen's ideas regarding technological determinism necessitate compilation and reconstruction. The reason behind such a necessity is that Veblen himself did not attempt to deliver a compact theory regarding social change. However, he meaningfully and systematically investigated the scope, role, and importance of science in human society, where technology is perhaps the most sought after upshot of scientific explorations (Veblen1919, 1898). Consequently, technological determinism has emerged as a coherent framework basically following from Veblen's writings. This theoretical paradigm is highly important to explain patterns of human interactions and behaviors, particularly in the vastly industrialized countries such as the United

States (Smith 1994). In the modern era, technology controls practically every aspect of human endeavor and enquiry. It cannot be denied that technology has a very important influence on human life since most of the primary achievements and constructs of human civilization are based on technological innovation and technology use.

Research Question

What is technological determinism?

Literature Research

Before directly delving into the intricacies of the conception of technological determinism, it is a good idea to understand what is determinism all about? In the book *Freedom and Determinism* (2004), the editors have characterized determinism in the form of an antonymous concept vis-à-vis the notion of freedom. Now it is indeed not possible to furnish a single and all agreeable definition of freedom. But in philosophy, determinism is a widely used term. Not only that, scholars have tried to categorize determinism as well as characterized it from various viewpoints. For example, moderate reasons-responsiveness (*Freedom and Determinism* 2004, p. 151) has been formulated as a theoretical paradigm that can be highly useful when explained even in the context of strict determinism with regard to guiding notions like ethical responsibility as well as limitations of real life. In fact, some contributors have advocated for a balanced approach between the strictness of determinism and the laxity of freedom by exploring different compatibilist choices in a systemized, scholarly manner (*Freedom and Determinism* 2004, p. 231).

Technological determinism is based on the proposition that technology has a powerful influence on human society, so much so that it can not only bring social changes but also control the long term socioeconomic behaviors and beliefs of the human beings (Smith 1994; Moore 1965). The theory has prime focus on a technology based approach, which marks technology as a driving force. This driving force may acquire characteristics of a pervasive influencer that can bring about a social change (Veblen 1919, 1898). The influential nature of technology might also be regarded as practically free of other disciplines and entities such as political organization, economics, culture, and even the society itself. Technological determinism has two principal ideas. Firstly, strict technological determinists believe that the trajectory of technology development follows a predictable locus which is independent of socio-political and cultural influences. Secondly, technological determinists state that technology has vast influence on society while technology itself is seldom conditioned by it (Adler 2006).

The most important characteristic of technological determinism is that it gives the opportunity to look beyond the horizons of typical reductionism. Instead of over simplification of the process of social change, technological determinism can be used to explore the complex dynamics of human and technology interactions. The institutional attributes inherent in human society cannot be neglected in studying the processes of social change as well. Technological deterministic approach helps the sociologist to understand the dynamics of social institutions in the light of modern technologies and their use. This feature of the theory has made it more important in the age of information technology and social networks in the global world. (Brette 2003)

Despite the fact that academicians like Moore (1965) have appreciated the idea of technological determinisms as a distinct form of theory aimed at explaining social change, the principals of the theory are looked at with somewhat scholarly skepticism. In fact Moore (1965, pp. 24-25) states that the social deterministic approach, as explained by this theory, has received an "alleged primacy" in the world of sociological scholastics. Yet, a certain degree of determinism appears to be necessary to solve the conjectures of social changes, especially when they unexpected, abrupt, and/or large-scale (Bottommore 1972).

It is true that the principal of determinism enshrined in a theory may restrict its scope to evolve and develop on its own. In attempting to leverage on reductionism, technological determinism thus emerges as a rigid point of sociological view. According to the strict followers of this theory, human society is regarded as incapable of developing its own socio-economic dynamics irrespective of technology change or technology use. Although it cannot be argued that technology has superior influence on the events as unpredictable as natural calamities like flood, earthquake, etc., proper technology use such as improved medicines plays a crucial role in determining key socioeconomic indicators like human life expectancy, health, nutrition, etc.

Furthermore, institutional investment and effort are necessary to facilitate innovation and discovery of new technologies. So the institutional characteristics of the society make it powerful enough to analyze its needs and devise new techniques to fulfill them. However, trends and trajectories (Dosi 1983) of technology research and evolution often emerge as more powerful than expected. And in such circumstances, technology itself may become a driving force behind social change (Brette 2003). For example, today's powerful social media and networks like Facebook, Twitter, etc. have helped people around the world to caste off cultural barriers and engage in widespread debates on different social, political, economic, academic, or technological issues with considerable freedom and ease.

According to Adler (2006), technological determinism has been utilized at several analytical gradients. At the broadest extent of sociological discourse, the theory has informed numerous analyses of changes witnessed in different socio-economic configurations. Processes like the social transition from feudal systems to capitalist democracies and changing patterns of labor structures cannot be explained fully without at least a partial but forceful implementation of technological determinism. Further according to Adler (2006), there are many other important theories of social change that draw inspiration and develop scientific basis with the help of technological determinism. In this regard, the element of technology in those theories is considered as a prime factor alongside other factors like society, labor theory, linguistics, etc. For example, several social scientists have attempted to explain technological determinism with the help of the concept of dialectical materialism as derived from Marxist worldview (Moore 1965). Another pillar of the technological deterministic theories is determinism, which tends to develop a framework of technological development with the help of the concepts of historical analysis and forecasting. However, Moore (1965, pp. 86-

87) appears to be highly critical towards such an interpretation of the theory and states that certain major variants of this theory must not be "exaggerated into a unique prediction."

General Discussion

Although writers like Adler (2006) have referred to the concept of technological determinism in a very direct and systematic way, the term determinism appears to have more affinity with philosophy than sociology. This point is proved if a researcher examines the various edited works and collections of essays related to this field written by distinguished scholars. The collection of essays and theses edited by H. Atmanspacher and R. Bishop is extremely useful in this regard (*Between Chance and Choice: Interdisciplinary Perspectives on Determinism* 2002).

If the term determinism is explored from a completely philosophical approach, then different perspectives from different fields of study can be discovered which explain or utilize determinism in numerous ways. This is why professionals from different fields such as management and technology can be benefited from a discussion on the philosophy of determinism. For example, there are many scientists who do not endorse or rely on research projects and theses that are overly dependent on non-empirical studies or relate with topics that generally fall in the category of humanities or inexact sciences (e.g. astrology, palmistry, fiction, etc.). Scholars like G. Nickel have attributed this kind of research and analysis approach to scientific determinism, where practical experiments and physical measurements are given a very high degree of importance (*Between Chance and Choice: Interdisciplinary Perspectives on Determinism* 2002, p. 33).

Scientific determinism has again been extended further to develop research approaches that can facilitate enquiry in relatively more multifarious topics. B. Misra has instanced the use of deterministic approach to analyze and solve problems in quantum mechanics, where conceptions like Heisenberg's Uncertainty Principle remain not only enigmatic but debated as well. In this way, determinism has applications in physics and chemistry too. Furthermore, B. Slife has elaborated the scope of determinism in studying clinical psychology, where place and time related issues are frequently found among most of the patients and psychiatric counselees. For more detailed information on these works (as related to quantum mechanics and psychology), refer to the book *Between Chance and Choice: Interdisciplinary Perspectives on Determinism* (2002, pp. 149, 469).

So in the realm of technological determinism, it cannot be denied that the concept of determinism, as used in the realm of various science subjects ranging from physics to psychology, can be utilized to solve issues related to research, analysis, and experimentation techniques. But how can this sort of utilization of determinism as a concept help in understanding the society better? Determinists generally advocate having a rigid approach toward research where experiments and exactness of measurements are extremely important. In such a state of affair, can a researcher use a determinism based research approach to study some branch of social sciences too?

Brinkerhoff et al (2008) provide excellent answer to the tribulations as mentioned in the previous paragraph. During the middle of 19th century, the concept of economic determinism emerged in prominence. Left-leaning social scientists in contemporary Europe were especially impressed with this concept. Brinkerhoff et al (2008, p. 6) have furnished a concise but informative note on economic determinism with reference to Marxist theory. In this way, determinism can be introduced in the realm of economics. And from this point, determinism becomes highly relevant in the subjects like political science, social work, and sociology too.

So, technological determinism can be regarded as a field of study that has emerged due to the combined effects of interdisciplinary research in different areas of intellectual enquiry. Even if a researcher avoids determinist approach in understanding importance of technology, he/she will have to agree with the fact that evolution of technology does play a very important role in human society. In the context of social change, this factor becomes even more emphatic and decisive. Technological capabilities can decide the course of history. For example, invention of steam engine can be regarded as one of the prime factors that gave rise to industrial capitalism. Invention of anti-malarial quinine can be regarded as an epoch making event that changed the very nature and scope of healthcare systems in the tropical countries. Advanced naval technology and navigation systems played a key role in Britain's success as a colonial empire. There are several other well known facts like these, which can be used to demonstrate the effect of technology on society in both regional and global contexts.

In this way, technology can be assumed to have a very important role in the development and evolution of modern human society. However, is this role of technology deterministic in nature? The answer to this question appears to be debated.

At one side, there are the scholars like Smith (1994) who hold that technology is a crucial driving force in the evolution and development of human society. On the other side, there are scholars like Bottommore (1972) who think that there are several other factors along with technology that can bring about substantial social change. Scholars like Adler (2006) appear to be in favor of a constructive discourse over the issue. However, the main problem and debate are around the rigidness of an ideally deterministic approach. In sociology, the factor of rigidness is highly problematic. There are various forms of determinisms that are already a part of the broader sociological discourse. And the best example of these deterministic views is that of economic determinism. According as this view, economic relationships are most important in explaining human society including the dynamics of social change (Brinkerhoff et al 2008). Therefore, if a researcher attempts to develop some kind of social perspective completely on the basis of technological determinism, he/she will be challenged by those who believe in other deterministic views such as that of economic determinism.

Possibly, the most suitable way of utilizing technological determinism for the purpose of sociological research is allowing limited flexibility. For this purpose, the rigid belief that technology is the most important driving force in social change must be given up. Deterministic nature of the viewpoint can still be maintained. If technology is regarded as one of the essential factors that bring about a social change, then technological determinism can be realigned in par with other viewpoints such as that of economic determinism. This can be termed as a compatibilist (*Freedom and Determinism* 2004, p. 231) stance, which maintains deterministic values as well as synchronicity with other equally influential views.

Conclusion

Technological determinism can be criticized on the grounds of excessive rigidity, reductionism, and simplifications of dynamics of social change. Moreover, it has several powerful and widely accepted competing perspectives. The most important sociological viewpoint that vies technological determinism is economic determinism. Both of these perspectives on social structure and change have their unique qualities and drawbacks.

However, the factor if technological influence and advancement appears to be increasingly inseparable from the doctrines that can meaningfully explain the different dynamics of modern social order in the industrial world. Technological determinism is thus an important framework that can be used to analyze the different relationships between human society and scientific technology. Consequently, technological determinism can be regarded as a very important theory of social change. With the advent of information technology, mobile phones, and various kinds of social networks, technology has profoundly affected the very way humans communicate between each other. Since the role of technology has thus become critical even in the realm of interpersonal communications, technological determinism can be used more effectively today. Given the rise of new technologies capable of revolutionizing different social processes ranging from genomics to politics, understating the relationships between technology and society is becoming more crucial everyday.

List of References

Adler P.S. (2006), Technological determinism. In: S. Clegg and J.R. Bailey (Eds.), *International Encyclopedia of Organization Studies*, New Delhi and Thousand Oaks: SAGE.

Between Chance and Choice: Interdisciplinary Perspectives on Determinism (2002), H. Atmanspacher and R. Bishop (Eds.), Charlottesville: Imprint Academic.

Bottommore, T.B. (1972), *Sociology: A Guide to Problems and Literature*, Mumbai: George Allen and Union.

Brette, O. (2003), Thorstein Veblen's theory of institutional change: Beyond technological determinism, *European Journal of the History of Economic Thought*, 10, pp. 455-477.

Brinkerhoff, D.B., White, L.K., Ortega, S.T., and Weitz, R. (2008), *Essentials of Sociology*, Belmont: Thomson Higher Education.

Dosi, G. (1982), Technological paradigms and technological trajectories: A suggested interpretation of the determinants and directions of technical change, *Research Policy*, 11, 147-162.

Freedom and Determinism (2004), J.K. Campbell, M. O'Rourke, and D. Shier (Eds.), Cambridge Massachusetts: MIT Press.

Moore, W.E. (1965), *Social Change*, New Delhi:
Prentice Hall India.

Smith, M.R. (1994), Technological determinism
in American culture. In: Smith L.R. and Marx L.
(Eds.), *Does Technology Drive History? The
Dilemma of Technological Determinism*,
Cambridge MA: MIT Press.

Veblen, T. B. (1919, 1898), Why is economics
not an evolutionary science? In: T. B. Veblen,
*The Place of Science in Modern Civilization and
Other Essays.* New Brunswick, New Jersey, and
London, U.K.: Transaction Publishers, 1990.

Notes

Notes